THE VERBAL OASIS
Through The Eyes Of Athel

By:
Sthembiso A. Shabalala

Published by **Athel Publishers**

Athel Publishers

Copyright © - 2019-20
All Rights Reserved Worldwide
No parts of this publication may be reproduced, duplicated nor transmitted either by electronic means or in printed format without permission of author/publisher. Copying of this document is strictly prohibited & any storage of this work is not allowed unless with permission from the publisher/author.

Dedication

On a personal level? This is dedicated to my family & friends. I hope they draw inspiration from my work ethic & start to work towards changing their lives.

And on a global scale, this is for the bookworms, the love-smitten, the crazy & embracing, the ones who allow themselves to feel but lack the voice of expression, the free thinkers & world changers. In essence, it is for us all. Yes, this book is dedicated to anyone & everyone that feels. I hope you take something from each piece & enjoy reading them throughout.

ACKNOWLEDGEMENTS

First, I would like to thank my then lover, who has shown me love & support throughout the process of writing this book. Thank you. Lots of love & light!

Then, thank my wonderful peers who have been pushing to get a book out of me. I am grateful for your energy. Here's to love, joy & prosperity for the rest of our living!

Love-Induced Bruises

Love me from a distance or love me on the low,
Because as soon as you confess it - I will most probably go
Did you not see that I'm broken when you saw me from a mile?
I have gone through the worst, recognise my crooked smile
They say abandonment issues do a number on us,
That is why we grow insecure & push away anybody who tries to love us
Question every move they make when they are not around,
Trust when it comes to them is nowhere to be found
But anyway, back to the actual story,
I am hard to love & to love is hard, I'm sorry
& I know somebody will be mad when they read this,
Doubt my care for them or ask if I'm really with them
This is just a piece of my mind, take your heart off when you read this,
Whoever feels threatened by this, I feel for them
This is just the other side of me who is afraid to take love chances,
& I am not flipping on anybody, I'm merely sharing my love-induced bruises

Sthembiso Ayanda Shabalala

To Whom It May Concern

Maybe you were right - we are not compatible,
If I had to be deeper me to you, I may not be comfortable
You are way too perfect, too real & incomparable,
I would attempt saying something about you, but I would just be lost in my own parable
I hate how I read between the lines, I misread them all
when they are nothing you draw at all
You are a straight one, you clearly rule down your draw,
& understand me very well, shade is not what I am trying to throw
Though I come with breakdowns, I do not mean to drag you down nor cause you frown,
& if anything, I never wish to offer you burdens to tow
I have a lot of things I need to you know… my hope is that we care enough to let us grow
I have not known you for long but within me you have grown,
Take care of this heart & keep steady that crown

Dark Age - The Black Age

Let me take you back to the age of our forefathers,
The super men and women who fought for us to see this part of life's end
Necks leashed on with chains & hands tied as prisoners,
Kind natives whose mistake was embracing in friends
Little did they know of the loathe coming in with these fremds
Pilgrims who sailed in selling things,
Saw the value of the land & decided to steal away its peace
White chicken who saw in them black baboons,
Good for nothing fools, only good to be tools
Detesting their colour so they strapped down their honour,
Forcing out their valour & forcing in their power
Seeing strong wise kings, attempting to weigh them down with the brand name 'niggas',
But that never stopped their true destiny- Kings of the world & the actual word is Negus!

Sthembiso Ayanda Shabalala

Silent Tears

Tears of a silent girl, broken as a child
No words for the days of old & has fear to confide,
Light shines her scars, so she seeks darkness to hide
None be aware of the screams in her mind, thus in lone she cries,
Maintains a smile everyday so her beauty never dies
The mirror knows her terror, four walls hold in the horror
The tale of her life began with a massive error,
Forced by an old hag to lay her down & bed her
Threatened with a loss of life should she ever sing,
Sight of the beast brings about tears & aching
He is known as the saint of the house, bread winner & king
Tears of a broken soul, a streaming river of a pretty face that is soaking,
An angel so sweet has been perverted by cruelty into becoming a bitter being

How Cold My Heart Is

I am too much of a sinning jerk, I do not know what judging is,
I do not really care about warm love, that is just how cold my heart is
Whether or not it is tough love, I just want it as raw as it is,
Not influenced nor tampered with - I take it the way it is
Give me love or hate, the difference is the same with me,
Because I know both feelings can consume you heavily
Much reason why I hardly pay mind to anybody hating me,
& whoever takes offence can go jump, really;
I'm just putting my thoughts on ink, sincerely
This is how cold this heart is, get the emphasis
& I hope this reaches eye and ear of all my deared friends & nemeses
Let them know who *Athel* is so they are clear on the deal,
Before my actual uplift & reception of the Skrill
Put them in light of the truth from the coldest depths of my heart,
So, they can quickly learn to accept me from the kindness of their hearts
I am writing about how cold my heart is because of my burning love for art,
This ice berg may be my own but for it to be this way, people played a major part

Sthembiso Ayanda Shabalala

The Woman I Should Marry

She really has to have viable brains,
I need her smart & confident like a queen in reign
She doesn't even have to read books,
All she needs is an enlightened mind - regardless of how she looks
She must put her potential to good use, not look for a man she can climb on & use
Retain good morals & never act loose,
Work for her own so she never experiences any form of abuse
This woman must take less than she gives
Not always expect something given to her, thereafter she leaves
Never steal my peace as it is done by thieves,
She can wear her make-up, nails & wear her weaves
But her soul has to be pure & clean,
Love with all she has & always calms me down when I am mean
The woman I am to marry ought to be a role model to our daughter
& show my son how his wife should be like by just looking at her mother,
The woman I will be chained to should be a winner

Moment Of Clarity

I sent a friend an e-book & told my old brother to read a book,
I believe in empowering family & friends, are you really shook?
Old folks envy my brain's mature, young lads crave my dress culture
These words are very real, do you need proof sure?
I am never trying to find anybody to mimic,
Because all of these beings are nothing but gimmicks
I am only trying to be the best version of my own self, keeping
in mind that not even the sky is the limit
Do everything in my might to make hard levels easy,
Just so I can snatch any opportunity & run with it
I have employed my drive to be the chauffer - that is how I stay driven
Each time I say things, nobody ever listens,
& hours ago, I said I do not believe in curses but do in blessings
Then I went on to say a man who knows white, surely knows black
I mean, would you ever know or appreciate blessings if you knew not curses?
Like typing on this white pad, how would you know that these letters are black?
We know no wrong if we are unfamiliar with the right
We can never tell it's dark if we have not seen the light, am I right?
This is the moment of clarity; may our imaginations run free of gravity, so embrace levity!

Scars

I have a body covered in scars,
The kind that deprives you sound sleep at night, cover your eyes
I am not ashamed of it, it is the most splendid by far,
A body engraved with memories, lessons, hurt & lies
I have flashbacks of every bruise;
I would cover them with ink, but those are not the kind of mementos I will to lose
You may see the physical but they run deeper than that, very spiritual
Thinking of it makes me a little emotional,
Lest you catch nightmares - may they remain mystical
I'm a stream of mystery, a new man with history,
Crowned with a crown of thorns & received with a song of horns
With all lessons I have learned, I still wonder where I stand,
Is there efficacy in all the knowledge I have earned?
I am far from impressing me, the journey is far from end
I have gained what I had needed, lost what for I was never meant,
These scars run deep... if you decide to dive in, ensure you do not sink

How I Survive

I gave out a lot of pieces of work in the name of practise,
But we long ran past that, now it is time to put it all to practise
Because in any case toleraters will most probably rate this,
& whoever's a hater will most definitely hate this
It is time I lifted up, put these words in poetry - recite & write it all up,
I never lay no word down when everything feels bogus
Though I am living proof you do not need drugs to be creative,
I art it all out without ever being deceptive
& this is not debateable, you can go argue with your clique
I turn a blank screen to an insight-filled one in a few clicks
How many years back did I last cry?
I let the pen spill tears of ink to make my loud miserable cries
You are curious on how I survive?
My pen also serves as a razor - cutting the inner pain out to keep me alive
Utilize my vocal chords to summon a brighter future to life,
I let it all out on paper record, that's how I survive

Smell The Coffee

I do not recall the last time I bought clothes, sacrifices;
I will keep doing my own thing until it all suffices
I have got no trust for these folks who feed me advices,
But pretty soon I will hit them with nice life surprises!
I do not hope for anybody to point at me,
When my craft lifts up & claim that they made me
I do it all on my own so nobody can own me
All the things I do, I do them to me & for me!
Lately my academic focus has been shifted, my head is tilted,
But I am a gift with numerous gifts, my passion is well-fitted
I feel disorder, who can order me order?
Whoever does so will be verily thanked with honour ...
Had to tell self, "fall back, run a bit slower,
Order your steps well & allow them to lead you without boarders
You are every second getting older, ensure your planning is accordingly proper,
You better wake up to smell the coffee before it's too late & all over...

Forest Mind

I strongly feel like nobody will ever comprehend my thoughts & emotions,
so I keep them to myself,
It is like drowning deeper than the actual ocean's depth, do not even wonder how I surf,
How I keep head above water just to see a day's sky
I have always understood that you need to first jump to ever fly,
Face & conquer all fears, don't be afraid to die
Dreamers are believers, Winners are seekers
So, believe in your dreams & forever seek victory,
We all have the liberty to speak life into our ideal lives, for a far better future
With writing as my remedy, my internal verbal therapy,
I intend on touching lives for the better, plant a seed of thoughts that bear fruit to happy
Still retaining the poetic protocols & its culture,
I keep it real with everything, only gunning at vultures
That await on dead situations & feed on dead visions
Dead presidential notes in duffle bags as the sole mission,

Those ones deserve the worst kind of termination!

Sthembiso Ayanda Shabalala

Battle Within

The things I am going through seem to have silenced me,
No retaliation of adversities outside, inside is where the violence be
When you are looking at me, can you see through my eyes?
Do not tell me about the smile on my face, within Is where the story lies
I keep dropping down, yet I am holding on tight,
What keeps me up is that I am treading on with a fight
To be bullied by life is not the reason why I am on this Earth,
So, I will proceed standing up for myself until I face death
I know this deep darkness is signalling breakthrough,
It is attempting to tell me bright light is coming through
May my plot be not lost as I advance for a better spot,
I will probably inspire with this story some day when I succeed
Because it is never over until breath is lost,
I might be feeling cursed at the moment, but I pray for Godspeed
Some may see me as dead weight, but I see myself as a seed,
That will continue to rise from the mud, despite how many times it has been buried,
& to anybody aware of my challenges - I might be asking
for help but I do not expect to be carried

For The Prince

This piece of work right here is dedicated to my son,
Straight from the depths of my being - it was not scribbled for fun
My little man will have to know a few things,
He must really know himself & all that he wants
Be aware of the coldness of the world & all that it brings,
And value what he has mentally & physically, lest he flaunts
The first lesson he must learn is respect,
Before he is taught to work for his own & never expect
Be assured from time to time how much he is loved,
I would hate to have him running around like he is emotionally starved
One day I want to pass to him wisdom like a ball,
Tell him whenever he is down, he needn't be afraid to crawl
So long as he is moving on, forgiving all wrongs;
Discover productive & healthy ways to deal with pain, even if it means venting on songs
Like his father, be a poet or writer maybe,
Or be extramural, just to lift off shoulder weight when it's heavy
Whatever he finds joy in, whatever he wants to choose,
I do not wish to be a typical parental figure, telling him what to pick or lose
I just want to always be there for him, be a father I never had,
Because having one or no parent, can damage the child so bad

Sthembiso Ayanda Shabalala

Letter To You, Self

Learn to celebrate your little victories when you can
& be the one who pushes you to your peak prime,
Be loyal to your hustle & keep going with or without a fan
Never let go of that confidence, even man requires his pride,
Just rock a smile along the journey to good life & enjoy the ride
This game of existence may sometimes feel like a fantasy,
However it knocks you down, remember that you are your own ferry
So, go on and make that magic… always remain fantastic,
If you believe only money will free you, then be its fanatic
Mind your own business if you value peace of mind,
Isolate from negativity, trust the process of your grind
Not even one soul is obligated to understand your or your hustle,
But after all, what is the world without a slight boggle?
You are who you believe yourself to be, there will be no end to that story,
Be good, honest, loving and forgiving of yourself
Never think low but high of yourself like a King heading to his glory,
I hope you sit down & take some time to read this letter to you, self

Loving You Wrong

Baby, I am truly sorry, I know that I am loving you wrong
I just don't know how to feel with everything going on,
& since I cannot call nor tell you in person, then I will lay it down in poetic form
Lover look... lack of care is not the factor, I know all this to you is not fair,
You have always been there on my lows & whatever pain I had felt, you ask for a share
It is all just heavy on my head, plus I am kind of feeling numb,
I am trying to show emotion to this, but the brain refuses to succumb
Please do not turn your back on me, I know you are in pain,
Can we talk about this? I want to be here with you
Even though I do nothing but cause tears to shed off like rain,
You mean an awful lot to me; do you have a clue?
Yes, perhaps I am having difficulties fully expressing my emotions,
Everything between us was going good & I toned down the motion
We don't even text as much as we did before because you feel I am disconnected,
As if you are alone in all this and you are feeling rejected
I have no words to justify my acts, I'm just feeling empty & that is blunt fact
I have tried keeping it all together but there is too much on my plate,
& do clearly understand me, I am not saying you are adding on the weight
All I ask of you is to bear with me until this all blows over,
I am loving you wrong & that I know, but please do not tell me we are over!

Sthembiso Ayanda Shabalala

My Light

Years before I needed no light because I was nyctophilic,
But when you came around in my dimmed life, it felt like magic
Before you came through, I was nothing but an abyss so dark,
I was a blacked-out candle, but you shared with me your little spark
I am grateful, really... I truly appreciate you,
I care so much about you even you do not believe that I do
But I can never blame you for not taking my word for it,
I mean, I always tell you how I feel yet behave the complete opposite
I may seem like a fool, my mind bids me to act cool,
It reminds me of the history I have went past, how much pain I have felt
How I wasted 5 long years of my life to a girl I loved in high school,
Back then emotions thought for me, repeating that mistake is one of my greatest frets
& I am not looking to make you suffer for someone else's wrongs,
I am only trying to explain to you where it all went wrong
You are my light, but this is darkness I must fight on my own,
& please do hear me clearly, I am not leaving you... no, I am not having you outthrown

Letter Of Royalty

I am on a mission to build me an empire,
I have a vivid vision of multitudes addressing me as sire
But to ever reach... I must lead me first,
Before I can even think of ever leading living being best
As we all have been told to give out what we expect to receive,
It is only right that I become the first recipient of whatever I intend to give
I am talking about affection, belief & reverence,
I am still after glory, I could care less about glow's appearance
I must respect myself if others are to respect the crown,
If my presence is not valued, then I need no renown
Whether or not I am known, that will never make me frown,
But as soon as I avail, they must know I am not one to back down
I stand for what I believe in, I thrive to stay winning,
& my chase is far from end, this is only the beginning
However it is taken, this is a letter of royalty,
Call it a stupid fantasy if you will, but this is my reality
I am who I believe myself to be, I got that ringing in brain,
& each time I close my eyes... I see *Athel* sitting in reign!

Taken For Fools

This picture sends out a clear message & it speaks multitudes,
It explains how education lays to waste our mental magnitudes
How is suppresses our actual selves and modifies us like A.I. beings,
Demolishing our diversity, making us seem like one thing
While the law makers are uneducated men who force the society to heed every set rule,
Enslaving us our whole lives from academic institutions to
jobs, all the way up to being debt fools
Seems to me like the system was meant to benefit its founding fathers,
The wealthy men who never reason with anybody unless there is a score to acquire
Making us believe that the only way to a happy & satisfying life is through studying,
But why do I not feel joy & satiety when I am forcibly buried in books?
I honestly think the word STUD-YING is short form of Students Dying,
We are just being taught how to slave for dreamers, that's how it looks
Given lessons of how to be a good employee to an employer,
But when you do a background check on your boss, he's less qualified than you are
Do not get me wrong, I have nothing against learning,
I'm a man who values learning, I just hate the system
I hate how they fool us into believing another's vision gives us meaning,
How they box our creativeness & talents just to serve another man's dream

My Hole

Allow me to draw you a picture of the hole I have inside of me,
I assure you, this is something that will always be a part of me
It goes deeper than a pit like a crack that can never be repaired,
It is more than just a line of damage, it bears stories that can never be shared
Tales even I can never recite to my own self when I'm alone,
Even the slightest memory can poke the wounds & leave me wet eyes prone
I guess you can call me a time ticking bomb since I carry pain that is latent,
Just one more strong hit from reality & I will be left with a deeper dent
I am not sharing this to receive emotions of pretence,
This paper pad is still my shrink, I am only venting on it, in my defence
Do not worry yourself of the cause of damage,
Just appreciate words that were turned into an image
The poetic brief projected from my scarred & wounded soul,
No matter how you look at me after reading this, just know your judgement will never make me whole

Prayer Plead

There are a lot of things I will to say to you, Creator
Not only say, but look up & ask you as a believer
Ought I write them all out now or wait for my moment of prayer?
Should I say them now in poetry form or just wait for later?
Dear, G.O.D, forgive me for what I am about to do, but things seem rather odd;
I have been praying for an abundant warmth in this life, yet the degrees
seem to be gradually climbing towards cold
Hoping for better things, believing I was born into the
flesh to live like an angel without wings,
But I truly do not comprehend why living feels like this
Like each breath I take obliges me to bear with all the misery life brings,
Are obstacles supposed to endure as long as this?
Help me get this: what use is there for 2 seconds of joy if
you live the rest of your days in misery?
Should I keep hoping for light while this darkness is clouding me?
& I do not wish to seem arrogant, but why do you never reply when I cry out to you?
Why are you so silent when I reach out to you?
These days nothing seems to be going my way,
I even had a break down last night, shedding tears while I pray
All that had me wondering if you really do live,
You are always quiet, say something for me to believe

It's Crazy

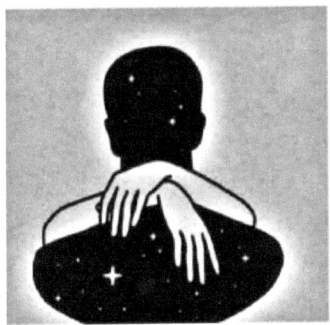

Child, I guess you are the one I have been waiting for,
All the others were just trial run, you are the one I was made for
Even though I do not believe in people being meant to be,
But I truly think your self was made just for me
Crazy, huh? How emotions can flip a pessimist instantly into an optimist,
How they can turn a heart-iced man into a harmless beast?
I am probably rushing things, reading between the lines that are not drawn,
Feeling like destiny found a way for me to smile again
You just need to understand that I am used to burnt grass, not this green lawn,
So, I always become hopeful in the sight of a bit of rain
I was told no one will ever take my rude self in,
Since everyone seems to want pure & perfect without sin
I can never be a saint - a dirtied soul never utterly gets clean,
& I swear I have tried being respectful, but I am utterly rude & mean
It seems you see none of the fouls people keep pointing at,
Like you look at me differently & I really love that
You give me all the respect & attention I need, you get me through the days,
I have been hopeless for a while now, so thank you for your grace

Sthembiso Ayanda Shabalala

Soul Sister

Best of love to all sisters, I mean soul sisters...
The ones you imbeciles see colour when you look at,
The very same ones whose value you murder, you cold-blooded killers
Allow me to revive their beautiful souls & image,
Instil in them the actual words to describe the contents of their mental books before turning the page
Ladies, I would tell you how pretty you are but that's cliché,
Rather I tell to take care of your crowns each day
You really do not need any validation to feel & be victorious,
I come from a family led by a single woman without a help of a man to carry us
Wear that exquisite skin as your own, it was made for you,
The cellulite & those stripes separate us men from you
You do not even need to hide majestic afros, ever
Wash off that powdery mask, have you any idea what is hidden under?
Do not dare be ashamed of your physique, you are dreams, lovers

The View

PERSPECTIVE

It is funny how society tries to line us up the same way,
How people think things will continue being the same everyday
How they try to define everybody's life with one term,
Attempt to line us up like well-packed products in in a firm
Turning a blind eye to the fact that we are all different in perspective,
Our brains are wired distinguishingly but they still try to paint us with one ink, irrespective
What do you mean whatever I'm doing is not right?
Are you not aware that my own rights are set apart from your personal rights?
I might be proficient utilizing my right hand, but someone else is best with their left
Why do we feel still threatened by everything that is unfamiliar?
If it is unknown it's of the devil, when it's common it's God's gift?
Stop being so mind-boxed and always be open to anything peculiar,
Explore every possibility, avoid having ideas that are fixed,
Embrace all differences; it may be a 9 to someone, but to another a 6
Clearing the air with this piece is the main objective,
I hope the smoke gets dealt with & we all stop being so oppressive

Sthembiso Ayanda Shabalala

I Need Answers

Life has given me a few hits, but I have never backed down,
Rose me high up just to smack me hard on the ground
It has made me feel blessed & gave me a smile, 2 seconds later making me frown,
I have been in pursuit of purpose & happiness; pain & lessons is all I found
I am not complaining though, I'm only becoming a better man,
Doing better than I did back then & being the best that I can
I have seen & went through unspeakable things as I grow old,
But none of these things have made me give in or even fold
I grow stronger everyday paying no mind to what who says,
Hated for my cockiness & detested even more when I self-praise
I am still wondering why believing in yourself is such a sin,
I mean G.O.D told us he is the greatest, are we not made in his image?
He told us no being is better than him, then why are we self-oppressing?
Why do we feel the need to please society by displeasing our own selves in this day & age?
Lest we forget that we were told & taught all that we know,
Reprimanded from thinking otherwise because it is not how things go
So, why ought I listen to anybody who has tried to box my brain, placed it in distress?
Somebody please tell me why I should feel blessed instead of cursed?

Blessed & Cursed

We are not given everything in this life,
We all have our deficits, I know the truth cuts deeper than a knife
Let us not act like we are perfect because we are not at all,
There are things each of us lack, we were born with shortfalls
One can be smart but without mere essentials to survive,
The other so dumb with a strong financial background to keep him above
One be given all limbs but grows up hungry in the slums,
The other without feet but is always holding a Mac between his thumbs
Sadly enough, we are all cursed & we are all still blessed,
Even if we argue about who is ugly or better dressed
It is an undeniable fact that no person is better than the next
We were all borrowed existence, there is only one host in this event,
& to be very realistic, we are all just privileged guests
So, let us start appreciating one another, you are not an island
You need me, I need you; to get where we wish to, we must hold hands,
Your uniqueness is required, you do not even need to blend

Sthembiso Ayanda Shabalala

Gene-Sis

Before you is a rare picture of our greatest gran,
With a wide nose, thick lips & darker skin
Proved to be one of the first of men to ever walk on these lands,
Said to have borne fruit to the whole of humankind
The famous anthropologists discovered and named her Luci,
The oldest fossil bones found, her face reconstructed to what you now see
You see... after recalling this history, a lot of questions flowed in
If Adam & Eve were the first to exist, then were their bones hidden?
How have we never seen tangible proof of anything we were made to believe in?
Has anybody, any intellectual scientist, found the location of Eden?
Then what is this I hear about the caucus nation being the aboriginal group?
If so, could they please explain to me why Luci resembles the black group?
Why does she not have a thinner nose, slimmer lips & a light complexion?
May I plead with anybody to set clear & give me an explanation?
& for what purpose was the word Genesis mis-explained
Genealogy of Isis is its true meaning, why was its true meaning changed?
Why were the Egyptians painted with history ink as evil, is it because
they were black people?
Is that why all they created & believed in was said to be lethal?
The only great nation to have built & achieved greater than the white colony,
Did they feel so inferior to decide to introduce white supremacy?

A Deeper Symbol

You may only prominently see 2 black hands meeting, to me there is a deeper meaning,
It is not just clenched fists colliding, but brothers & sisters uniting
5 fingers being singular reaching out to the other one
Sharing strength with its kind, assuring them they are never alone,
Just like one fist risen high up is a symbol of every black muscle
Both male & female, there is no man without a woman,
I know we are now segregated so we refuse to hold hands
But we need to work together to execute even greater plans,
Conquer in our division & excel where we stand
I am aware to most people a greeting formality is all that it is,
An alternative of a hand shake, something done impromptu
& I'm pretty sure nobody notices how profound this gesture is,
It is like every being for another, from the concept of Ubuntu
Something the born-frees are not familiar with,
But we are not there; that's for another day, back to the blood touch
KA! A spiritual part of the soul in Egyptian mythology which survives after death,
KA! A critical part of a people in the African history which lives without search
So, when you see a negro on the streets, give them love that they need,
Hit them with head nods, give them fist bumps & wish them Godspeed

My Holed Self

Lately I have been feeling like there is a hole on my chest,
Like I am missing a piece of me; this feeling is the worst
Feeling incomplete when you have no idea what could be missing,
Unknowing whether it was lost or was never even there in the beginning
It is pathetic feeling & I want nothing more but to erase it,
But first thing's first - I need to uncover what causes it
Is it lack of external affection or just lack of communication?
Some lack of external attention or just lack of self-appreciation?
On which side could the dilemma be, in or outside of self?
Am I missing a piece of me physically or mentally?
What could it be, friends? I am in dire need of a little help,
If you have an idea, help me discover what my loss be
Because I truly cannot live my life like this,
This thing depresses me, it robs me of my bliss
I try my best to keep head above water, but it always finds a way to drown me,
I do not know what I should do with it anymore, honestly

Celestial Body

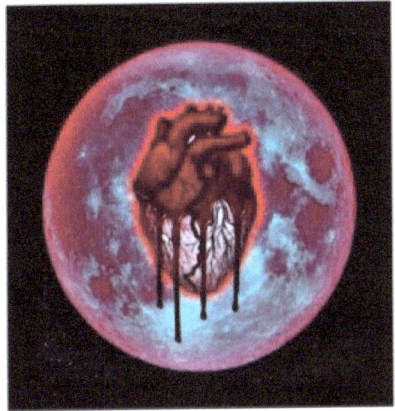

I have been complaining of no love when I know I exist without heart,
I took it out for an ache breather, but heart & I had a drift
He could not remain idle, so dear heart left for a trip,
I was too busy with mind business, so I did not see him leave
He left niggy dry, sucked all the love out to the last drip
Psych! That is just a little bluff tale I tell whoever wants to be with me,
I get a little pretendingly emotional when telling it, since they call for my honesty
Honestly? I threw my heart to the skies, if you are in need of it make a wish,
It will probably decide to fly into your chest mimicking a shooting star, like swish!
It is roaming on the cosmos like a heliacal planet,
While staying in tune with granny moon, mother earth's parent
Lately I have been unruly; believe me, I know what is going on,
I am on a paradigm shift & it is confusing lie believers who are trying to find something to hold on
& there's been no luck in attempts to break me & my beasts apart,
That is why I remain drawn to Sin, blame it on my Celestial Heart

Sthembiso Ayanda Shabalala

Black Reform

I do not mean to poke old wounds, but I must remind you of the past,
Remind you of where we are coming from as a Nation - we have been through the worst
Humiliations, castrations, misrepresentations, slavery,
Executions, exclusions, mis-educations, cruelty & poverty
But this is not when our beautiful phenotype began its existence,
We have had amazing accomplishments as Africans
With capitols like Ethiopia & the Great Egypt,
Where the civilization ideology was originally born, before they stole it
It was thieves like Alexandra their great, George Washington,
The Rothschild, Charles L'Enfant & the likes of Thomas Jefferson
To name a few of a zillion hippies who took advantage of our kindness,
Pretending to be good friends while having intentions of vileness
Infiltrated our continent & staged a grand charade,
Played us in plain like anime characters in an arcade
Now this the most crucial part of history,
Not the one where they are the face of a deity
The Son of G.O.D under the caucus skin,
Said to return as the Saviour of melanized skins
But anyway... that is a story for another day,
For now, let us focus on coming up with solutions to pave our own ways
We must re-inform & reform our people,
Tell them when you are brought to this world, you are not born evil
We need to unite if we are to completely have our freedom,
Therefore, love & respect are paramount in the process of regrouping
Leave your personal agendas out the door & come in with wisdom,
There is too much work to be done, there is no time for playing

Enough Is Enough

Brothers & sisters of the black house,
I scribble this piece as a concerned black child
I pray it reaches your senses or close enough to touch each blouse,
Because what I am wearing up my sleeves is a verily tarnished pride
Why do we find great grief in protecting any one of our own?
Acknowledging other races' superiorities but mocking another melanized fellow when he is rocking his crown?
I do not intend to be amusing, this must come to an end,
We are so divided, filled with hatred that we call an Afrikan from another country with every foul name but a friend
I do not mean to sound racist, but every race is united,
Supporting each other - sharing every opportunity granted
It is time to stand together & stop throwing shade,
Our intentions are already painted dark, dignities made to fade
I pray every black child goes through this & feels revived or inspired,
This is for everybody with dark genes, whether they call you black or coloured!

Sthembiso Ayanda Shabalala

Encoded Affection

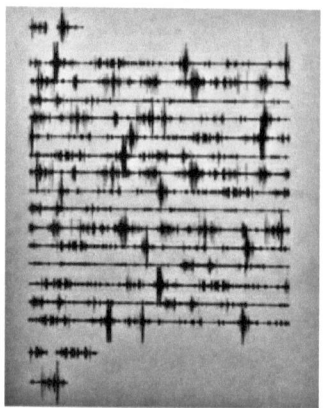

Dearly beloved, I have something I would love to share with you,
While you were sleeping at night, I was up all night thinking of you
Tossing & turning... my memory bank kept feeding my mental vision images of you,
So, I just opened up my paper pad & allowed my heart to go on about you
The letter is in love wave font, only a special heart like yours can decode it,
But you need to be on its level of frequency if you are to roger it
Because if not, then our hearts can never really be in sync,
There will be communication glitch & this relation-ship might sink
& there will be no turning back once the tides hit us,
Have your heart's frequency in check or it will be woe unto this
This is a letter written with complete & utter honesty,
It is meant to deduce if you and I are meant to be,
An emotional context that resembles our intimate analogy
A pour out of heart; I am frankly hoping you take a sip,
So to let it fill you up with my pure affection to the brim
Do not ask me what the passage entails, no do not make go deep,
Just take it, go saviour it & allow destiny to match our hearts' dreams

Religious Puke

I do not mean to look down on your morals & beliefs in discussion of this matter
& I am not letting my perspective out because I feel what I believe in or know is better,
Freeing our black humanity is the only intention of this letter
This is for my people who are unconscious to the psychological & spiritual warfare,
Imposed on the aware, unaware & even the ones who do not really care
Mental emancipation requires a lot of truth;
If we are to unshackle the chains, we must run back to our roots
Stop pledging our allegiances to deities that oppress us even more,
That mind screws us into submission & keep us on the floor
Regardless of the prayers & soul sacrifices - we suffer all the same,
A powerful people without sense of their strength & we are very clueless on who to blame
Since our history was stolen away from us to create fiction,
Cutting us off our roots like umbilical cords off a new-born's navel centre
Scrambling our past to influence our future, in actual proper diction,
Like a foetus being brainwashed while still in a belly through the placenta
The soul only grows wise this pure experiences & knowledge,
& ignorance commits more homicide in the days of this age
Let us seek to know & comprehend self - overlook the rage,
This is for the Pan-Africans... if you are not one, you may turn the page

Sthembiso Ayanda Shabalala

Book Tale

If you ever wondered where I get sense of peace & belonging-
Look no further, it is books that got me where I am standing
Yea, within a pile of verbal-inscribed leaflets packed with wisdom,
Is where I find this profound composure & mental freedom
This is the place where I found my power & might,
Shifting my paradigm to the 3rd eye of my sight
While freeing my mind to see beyond futile battles,
There is not chain on my hands & arms, thus I keep riding that saddle
Riding life like a knight on horse, the pain is mightier than the sword,
I therefore hold it straight up to help me fight my grave wars
So, seeking knowledge in these pages is smartest is accord,
The best narratives in the best kind of writing that history could record,
Give me lesson of how to live life I can truly afford
Now I physically & spiritually practise all forms of my awareness,
Secretly conspiring against secret societies that threaten my darkness
I'm at long last seeing the world for what it truly is,
A well-orchestrated play written in ancient scrolls
Scrolls that lay possession of devious men who just slaughter,
Ordering red guns to fire straight at the ethereous sons & daughters
But no more digressing, this was merely a tale about my lovely books,
They sharpen up my mind & keep me standing tall on my boots
Unbox my vivid thoughts rendering me smarter than any crook,
Turn off that electronic device for a minute & read an old school book

Emotionless Thoughts

I know G.O.D has never said a word to you - you have always assumed,
But you cannot lose faith in anything at this point, you need to resume
If you cannot have faith in your prayers, then it for your friends & family,
I am pleading that you do it your loved ones, niggy
Just try to make those ends meet to survive the days,
Hang in there & never lose hope- it is all just a phase
Do not burn potentially permanent breakthroughs for ones that are temporal,
Do not be pressured to act stupidly, pain is never eternal
For that reason, whatever you do... never shelter it,
Do not allow it to cloud your judgement, see through it
& if it weighs you down, find ways to crawl on,
Take it a day at a time until the heavy burdens are gone
Stay enlightened & think your way out of that pit,
Remember life is not a dice, so do not take any chances
Stay loyal to your grind to secure your take at the primacy sit,
Do not be shaken by a cold war, be flexible to all changes
I know you are overwhelmed with fear, but do not yield to feelings,
Always have a clear mind to think logically - that is how you will grow up & stay winning

Be Vigilant

Not everyone is there to help you; Some are just pretty front looking to trip you,
Others are a trap to those who wish you could pull through; but as soon as you reach the pinnacle, even the two-faced claim they had your back too
It is very amusing, huh? How your oppressors are always there to ensure you never go far?
How they are so gifted at covering their true characters?
Deceive you into believing they hope for you nothing but the best,
But just as soon as life takes toll, they turn out to be the worst?
Yea, there is nothing much to it, that is just how life goes,
& if you have never learnt about it, you are still to be sat on desk rows
Because like school, it is a lesson we all ought to fly via,
I am not saying never trust anybody or treat everybody as a liar
Be vigilant, learn to read people's vibes about you by reading their energy
The kilojoules should be galore if you are to them what is priority,
Stay loyal to your read & true colours will be revealed, eventually

Head Handy

We were given existence & we are expected to build it up,
Not just procreating, but also constructing without stop
Maintaining the growth & change since it is an infinite evolution,
Should the change remain stagnant, there will be life without emotion
So, um... let us work on ourselves, engineer our capital software,
We are what our minds state; Yes, we reflect what is in there
If you pay dirt to your mind, mud will be your fare,
If you are only depositing in it negatives, then life will not feel fair
But if the thinking is appropriate, so will be your reality,
Your most prominent thoughts manifest, that is what the truth be
You were not born with a manual because of your mental potency,
Your life is your own, you best decide what you want it to be
The universe always works in your favour, just say your command,
No, I mean mentally... your focus is what you are to find
If turmoil is all you think of - only chaos is going to arise,
& if complaints are all you are used to, nothing will ever suffice
Drill drive on your head screws until your internal is tight enough,
Connect those wires, make your light shine bright enough
Slave for your vision & the mission will one day be accomplished,
But if you remain in your comfort zone, you will be living in anguish
Take care of your head; it is time to get handy,
The only way to get you blowing, is if you start getting windy
This lesson might be feeling cliché, but some require this reminding,
Most of us do not have their heads right, thus some lessons need rewinding

Pro-Black

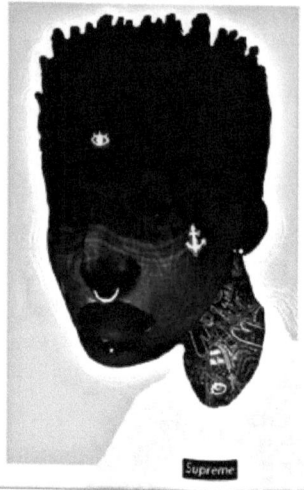

I'm pro-black, I love that I am black,
Melanin mixed with light - I am that
Darkness woven king in his Atheldom,
He who reigns mighty & supreme with his wisdom
Nappy hair as the crown, goes bald if he wants to,
Ever caps hide his 3rd eye... he never flaunts too
With an anchor around his neck, but spiritually on his left cheek,
That reminds him to be humble & grounds him when he speaks
His nose broader than your red necks' will ever be,
Lips bubbled up, thicker than anything you will ever see
Passion flows harmoniously with the verbal sense that he pukes,
Shares knowledge & bears a spirit nobody ever dares to rebuke

Sapiosexual

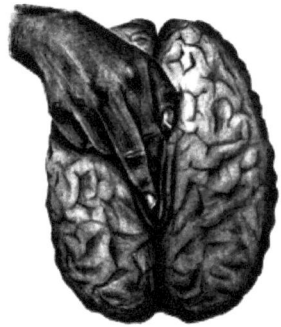

There is great pleasure I get from interacting with an intelligent mind
I am a sapiosexual; intelligence attracts me, it makes me feel alive,
It is something like getting foreplay on my corpus callosum, like clit thrive
So play away, baby... go ahead & ignite my bright brain,
Light it up & make me feel that enlightenment shower like the rain
Word play is fore-way, digital play our way & money is our prey,
May we scheme & plot all day and night to make paper bills come our way
& if it involves the world we live in, we are conscious to the core,
Intelligence that mind screws with reason, never to settle a score
If she never stimulates my mind like that, she may never come,
It is a different kind of coitus I am yearning for, no interruptus
One where neuron-firing thoughts are shared & it feels too awesome,
If some mental connection is involved in this, nobody can ever separate us
An attraction that surpasses the physical will withstand vultures,
The envious freaks & every one of these affection doubters
Beauty & curves can tempt me, but they can never keep me there,
A beautiful mind is what attracts & keeps me, to clear the air
I am sucker for brains of women that are overly confident,
Believe me you, a secured woman is nothing but the best

Sthembiso Ayanda Shabalala

T.C.O.M.H.

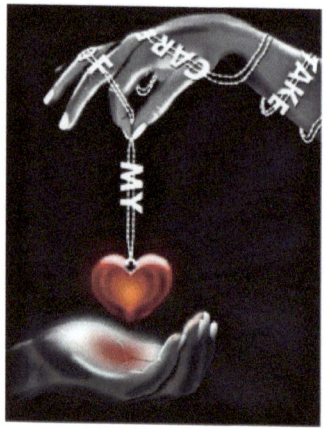

I was given a heart & I was pleaded not to break it,
Begged in heart-felt sense not to shutter it
"Take Care Of My Heart", she whispered softly in my ear,
"I want to grow old with you, despite all this fear
You strike me off as a special kind of casanova, but I am willing to let us try,
Dare not play me, you know how I easily cry
These boys put more than a dent on my heart;
So do not do me the same way, please do not tear me apart
Or the girl you will be fooling around with will be lost,
& all of your pillow talk promises will be terribly crushed
& all before you know it, she will be turned into ghost,
& all your stupid fantasies about her will be tragically smashed
I am giving you my all right from the start,
Love me & Respect my presence in your life; again, take care of my fragile heart!"
Those are the words she uttered while holding me tight
I listened with my eyes closed while my face lit up,
I felt like a lost toddler who has just found his light

My Beautiful Rose

My beautiful rose says I am breaking her heart,
Says I was never ready for commitment, I am slowly losing her trust
Neglecting her everyday like she does not even exist,
Texting & calling with no reply like I am deceased
She thinks causing her pain is something I am having a hard time to resist,
Like whenever I see her shedding tears, I feel very pleased
Like everything to me takes priority but her,
Like her body is all I ever wanted & then stop pretending to care
Asking me if she is ever going to be enough,
Demanding to know if I only wanted a few nightstands or a wife?
Am I taking her seriously or I just want somebody to laugh with?
Somebody to play with, have sexual relations with & do away with
Baby look, if you are reading this… know that I am sorry, please accept my apology;
I do not neglect you intentionally, I just have too much on the plate before me
You are the only flower I am attracted to, like a bee in pollination -
You keep my head buzzing all day even without communication
You swept me off my feet, you have been enduring all of this bull's shit
I owe you all that I can possibly offer, even now I grind to see you live best
Listen, spikey killer, I love you from your roots to your petals,
I am keeping distant all because I am stepping on my success pedal
For now, all you want is my attention… but as time goes, poverty
will be the major cause of our quarrels

YDNCM

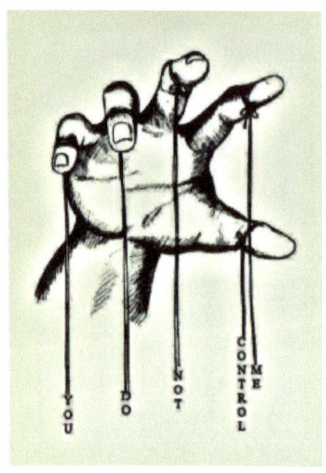

This is for the system maintainers, You Do Not Control Me
I truly am now a free man, as if You Never Really Reached Me
But I see my negros in the streets still shooting in the dark,
Claiming to be underdogs yet they never even bark
Sedating in the domes hoping to be a slightly bright,
But I am off that, let us talk about the ones who only favour the light;
The structures at the top that keep oppressing other people,
Though the subjects are not really conscious to the evils
Pretending to be writing their own sequels,
To their surprise their demise was an agreement made official
Eugenics was founded to decrease the world's human population,
The ones dimmed poorest & weakest are discussed unfit for new evolution
Force-feeding them lies about their strong & pure phenotype
The misinformation they ingest declares their minds fit for homicide,
This is a brief passage to the elite- I am not in your shackles
& this is not said out for the sake of hype

New Beginnings, Part 1

I am looking to start over, embrace that young me is now older,
Quit my old teenage ways & start realising with every breath taken, death is drawing closer
Time for playing games ran out for me a long time ago,
It is high time I stopped avoiding adulthood & just grow
Two decades & 2 years is what I am reaching next week,
So I need to keep on the work ethic that I am on to reach my personal peak
The best way to have a grass that is greener is to burn the old one,
Setting all my old dirty ways ablaze & building on greener pastures is all I ever want
Paving a different way for myself, little me would not get this one,
He truly would never understand, I am in a different state this current moment
But that is a story for another day, this is what I am trying to say -
Destruction is rather crucial for elevation, it is one of the old ways
History has had a restart quite a few times,
Like a small wipe out to create a generation that follows one lime
New beginnings are of utmost importance in this day & age,
Burn it all down to the ground if need be & enjoy the flame
watch on your way to turn the page

New Beginnings, Part 2

Now that we have turned the page, I am taking a different turn,
A whole new direction in this life, the old had to burn
I sowed this prophecy in the spiritual realm about a year ago,
I did not realise when I was planting how deep the seeds would go
But now that I took note, it is head-on with the plan,
A start of new beginnings & I will fulfil all that is on my wish-list, no matter the time span
I will live a life of passion from this day to my death day,
No more feeling chained & enslaved while hoping for better days
Taking charge of my existence, no more morning-waking resistance,
There now ought to be a huge distance between me & grievance
Did away with unhappy thoughts about what I get up to be about,
Made way for happier ones - not paying any mind to whoever's doubt
Radical changes implemented on my living - I feel so reborn,
Even though when everything hardly made sense, soul felt worn out
But as soon as I reflected on my previous year & writings, all the worry was gone,
I ploughed & planted wishes on higher dimension, now I am seeing a sprout

Lost Angel

Torn between believing & losing all hope,
Unknowing if, without her angel, she is ever going to cope
He was everything she ever wanted, her very own heaven & home,
But now that he is gone, what other man is fit to head her dome?
So many years wasted, more than 5 years, forever was never tasted,
Now she thinks of life as a pessimist & she is feeling neglected
Nobody deserving of her heart – she is closed from all proposals,
Good Kings with great minds sent straight to chance denials
A beautiful soul with crooked thoughts is what she has become,
Dark & twisted in her mind, her head is never calm
Even the trees she started blowing fails to make the peace come,
Instead, they induce vivid imaginations that cause her to see him melting off her palms
Pill-popping no longer sedates her nor numbs the pain
If pillows could talk, they would share a very wet story,
Because every night she lays her head tears fall off like rain

Sthembiso Ayanda Shabalala

Nubian

This is for my information freaks, all my knowledge seekers,
The black men & women who are curious of some truth pertaining real history about us
Nubia is an ancient kingdom in the valley of the Upper Nile,
A river that currently borders Egypt & Sudan for a mile
Nubian refers to all direct & indirect indigenous Afrikan descents,
A mixed population, diversified like South Africa is at recent
One of the great regions where civilization was brainstormed on,
With existence that runs back 2500+ years before Christ was even born
Damn right! The black nations were the 1st kind to be civilized,
The very 1st to develop modesty & class but the past was revised

To alter the way the tan saw themselves, propaganda was utilized,
Brainwashed into believing they are savages & it stays televised
They are verily demonized, even their traditions are painted evil;
All their beliefs shunned, customs instilled in their heads to be lethal
Now self-hate comes naturally, projecting it towards each other,
Families become torn without effort due to violent fathers
Mothers remain ignorant, all they are ever concerned about is looking lighter with longer silky hair,
Kids starve, going to school with old uniforms but they still show no care
But can we put much blame on our people? The scars run deep,
It is generational damage, you cannot teach wisdom you do not keep
If the parents are affected, children get affected automatically
I mean who else teaches life to us other than our parental guardians?
This is not a superficial dilemma, people are dented psychologically; some inherently
Since elders have lost all hope, let us work on the kids & do the best that we can,
Now that we know the cause of damage & pain, let us think therapy
to move forward & formulate a working plan

My World

Welcome to my world, where love is mere formality,
Where giving affection to the vast results in a fatal penalty
This is the dimensions where giving hate is better than handing love,
An existence where jealousy & detest work hand & glove
In this place being good is a sin, it is even worse if you win,
They say you think you are better as soon as your life takes a spin
Changing for the better while attempting to advance the hood,
They take you for a fool even if it is for the greater good
Here regrets are brought in by sympathy, your good heart's empathy,
Considering others comes with ache, furthest thing from eupathy
You can call it the belly of the beast, like we were born swallowed,
Eaten alive, neither of us is a saint, we are all unhallowed
Well, the righteous do exist this side but with a little taint,
Priests walk around snowflake garments with a bit of paint
Permanently marked on their souls by the adulteries they commit,
When standing on the alter, preaching to a very cold lot
That hardly feel his utter, words reaching very odds parts
They bear no fear & shed no tear – religious revivals have lost plot,
Faith is shedding off like doves of peace tearing off a beautiful heart

Sthembiso Ayanda Shabalala

Azania's Tale

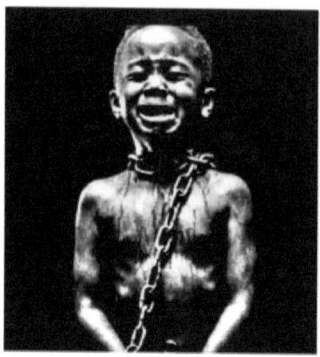

My name is Azania, I was born and raised in Jamaica,
I was twelve years old when I was taken from my home in Africa
They stole me from my parents & took me to a place I have never seen,
Shackled me in chains; told me this the luckiest I have been
Told me I am a waste creation, but I will be put to better use,
Before I grew even further to live whatever sorry life I will choose
"Your kind does not deserve to exist... Silence, you little rascal!"
Said the man in a black suite, verbalizing it all with disgusted facials
A well-renowned pastor, who is known as a good humanitarian,
Loyal to his country & brotherhood, plus a former militarian
So, I am asking as a human... what does it take to be one & be valued?
As I was branded savage before my experience of bad & good?
Before I could even tell between being scolded & being amused,
I was already sent on hard labour to milk cows & chop wood
I never understood why I am being mistreated, is it the colour of my skin?
The absence of my biological parents? The white one is never even pinched for any sin
So, what exactly did I do to deserve this kind of treatment?
Their kids are playing & learning without any kind of punishment
While I am locked inside a farm to slave off for their family
I am 16 years of age today & I have never felt what home
is... never had anybody to love me,
Tell me, is that how life ought to be?

Free Yourself

Free yourself from formalities & follow your own mentality,
Think your own thoughts & focus on your beautiful energy
Do not be typical with your existence, be proud of your uniqueness,
Even if you are the only fish of your kind, flow on & be relentless
Whether or not they understand you – you do not exist to clear enigmas,
If anybody speaks ruin to your name, give out a cold shoulder
Block any kind of vile vibe & dare not feel any guilt,
Just take steps towards your own course, you need not follow suit
Navigate this life with a clear mind, avoiding imitations,
Looking beside you instead of the mirror only brings about limitations
To some it all ends below the sky, while some of us consider the cosmos,
Our brains work differently & they all bear distinguished flaws
Sounding cliché is unintentional, but someone might need to read this-
Run your race without competing & allow your thoughts to emanate,
You are what your mind dwells upon, you already know this
Nobody holds the guide to your living, so why emulate?
Unchain your powerful mind from the habits of society,
Autonomy is all I am trying to instigate;
Let us begin today to be free at thought & evolve indefinitely

Sthembiso Ayanda Shabalala

Celestial Impact

Gazing at the cosmos, fascinated by its order & making,
Moreover, the peace it bears & all its exquisite adorning
Analogous figures floating on an ethereous vacuum,
A breath-taking mess above like ceiling reflections within a dark room
I believe in all the universe is & the forces it exerts upon us,
How we all carry the astronomy that is high aloft like Uber-stars
Celestial bodies enclosed inside a deific mega atom,
Earthlings that evolve better than any creature you, at present, fathom
This is the kind of knowledge you never find without search,
A sky bird that roams around yet without effort you seldom catch
An esoterical awareness like the Orion's belt asterism,
Perverted in scrolls to create a historical dysphemism
Hidden in plain sight but you only notice it when digging deeper
Looking into the real reality. Avoiding intelligence's absenteeism,
The ignorant arrogantly attempt to scratch off the truth like lepers
But a matter of fact is that I am a vessel of the universe
With my mind the milky way galaxy, igniting up planetary sparks,
Each time ideas illuminate on my spiralling brain like objects in the ethereous dark
A little more like astrological models entangling on the phi,
What are we, you ask? A stack of tetrahedrons & our minds ascend as we die
Different chapters of the same tale that form a Divine plan,
We are a human race 1st before dividing into different phenotypical races & clans
Stop the segregation & unify to harmonize as the Supreme being intended;
Rocking manipulative tactics & oppressing each other is redundant

Mentalism

All is mind & mind is all – the universe is mental,
Realise the power you enclose & deal with life's detrimentals
Mentalism is a doctrine that believes the physical exists because
of your cerebral awareness,
It follows a notion that says you may utilize your mind to manifest greatness
If you can think it, you can believe in your own self & achieve it,
Speak it into existence and act your part, all shall follow suit
You retain all the tools to prosper, just switch to your mentality,
Start being responsible of your reality with this ideology
& quit actively waiting on deity you will one day blame,
Take charge of your living, put an end to the blame game
Be one with the universe... "As a man thinketh, so is he"
Think appropriate thoughts & decide what you want your life to be
You bear a great deal of potential, all that is left is to discover,
Uncover mysteries of your being and lead yourself better

Sthembiso Ayanda Shabalala

Solitude

I think I might feel comfortable with such high altitude,
Where I can be far from everything & be in solitude
Where I will not have to deal with any stupid remarks & negativity,
With nobody to complain about my sincerity & sensitivity
I think I can do pretty good looking at the constellation,
I can even have a sound mind due to meditation
As long as I have good music, books & my pad to write on,
I would be splendid & I am sure nobody would miss when I am gone
I know people love you when you are no more,
But while you are still alive, they despise you to the core
Just like now, after reading this a few of them will not really feel good,
Since I prefer facts & truth, I do not care about their moods
If I could, I would truly take off from all this,
Go to a place where I will not face most of this
No, I am not wishing to escape responsibility,
I know I am where I am today because of my pure fidelity
I just need time to reboot & re-root,
Find inner peace & my ground to stand tall on my boots
Just to bring my head back on my shoulders & revive my pride,
I want to elope by myself to a desolate galaxy
Explore, think & be inspired, I do not want to hide;
I need time off from all earthly creatures, frankly...

Own Team

I still find peace in my solitude & I swear it is not bad attitude,
I promise you, I do not it for isolation, it is for my mental fortitude
I take pleasure in gazing at the sky, just starring at the moon,
It makes me feel alive because I know I will be ascending soon
No disrespect to the ones who think I do it for attention,
It is for my own progression, being the centre is not the intention
I am who I am, and I will never be down on my knees for it,
Unapologetically so, solitary states give my vision a better exhibit
Ironic, right? How being kept from seeing the world gives me a clearer perspective?
How a silent place & unoccupied space renders inner me expletive?
How whenever I feel helpless, I need time to myself to re-root,
Reconnect with my within to contemplate on how else I can loot
Back my sanity in the aftermath of spiritual & mental warfare,
When my inner beings quarrel about who is fit to adjudicate for my welfare
I am probably the most expressive man, yet I never confide –
I talk to myself more than anybody & I give me better advice
Narcissistic tendencies, I know… but my business resides best inside,
Having a human confidant in this harsh world is hardly wise
I am therefore better off facing my trials & tribulations on my own
I have been fighting my own wars since kindergarten, now I am grown;
I do not mean that I do not need anybody's hand, I just battle better alone

Sthembiso Ayanda Shabalala

Info-Transcendence

The more books I read, the more conscious I become,
See the world as it truly is, all that is a mystery to some
The more you seek knowledge, the more you lose yourself,
But also, as it all gets revealed you grow addicted to the shelves
Information is In-Formation, indulging in it feels like Re-Incarnation,
A layman's personal rebirth, just like a caterpillar's detonation
The butterfly connotation metaphorically meaning growth,
A transition of knowing forces you to go through phases without oath
But you need to have a teachable spirit in order to learn,
It can re-programme your head, make you think critically & better discern
Unlock new chambers in your brain so you better observe,
Get to the mental level you deserve, never allow your mind to starve
This is how you feed it, this is what it devours & to it, it is edible;
So, keep loading in data whether digital or legible
If you ever want to transcend, take every necessary step,
Informative pages are steppingstones crucial to ascend to the top
Make time for a little read in your phones & your iPads
Or find a hardcopy if you find it hard to cope with technology;
Just add some value to your brain, you know the power is in your hands

Peasant-King

It does not matter how they, but how you see you,
It is not where you start but where you are heading to
Not your physical appearance but your mental potency,
Yes, my good friend... you are who believe yourself to be
Even if you have not reached yet, vision is what matters most
See yourself as you envision and work towards getting close,
Be the product of your own dreams, the captain of your own boat
& do not worry yourself about the current state, keep pushing
A race is never begun at high speed, respect humble beginnings,
Focus on the win & regard blocks on your path as curves of learning
I know you are yearning for your break, all in due time,
Stay grind loyal & trust the process, I swear you will yield a dime
Do not allow yourself to slack, consistency is truly paramount,
Invest your might in what you love & stand for or reroute
If there is no passion nor belief in what you do, rather dismount,
Hitting a few walls & snares does not mean you are down & out
We all receive a fair share of stumbling blocks & there are no discounts,
I hope you take my words into account & make your efforts count

Sthembiso Ayanda Shabalala

Born Ready

It has been engraved on my genome, I was born ready,
However rattling the world is, I was taught to remain steady
Added to the lessons was that no trash can was made for a human,
And that respect is for us all but do it better on the life veterans
I am talking about the elderly; it was never a two-way street,
You either respected the grown or get taught a lesson
& you had to care for your neighbours, give them a family treat,
Even if life just recently hit you on your knees, stand tall on your feet
When you eat, remember the starving & needy around you,
It is one hand for another & humility will always ground you
No man is an island, you need troops to be a Sergeant,
Whatever leadership traits you retain, to be King you need peasants
I hope that makes sense… but anyway, back to my tale,
Fought grown battles as a child; if life is a bull, I grab it by the tail
Climb up its back, grab its horns & create a fortune from its saddle,
I always grab the bull by the horns, turmoil never made me settle
I am a man who believes in fighting for what you think you deserve,
A man who takes ache & failure as nothing but a learning curve
With an enduring soul that is very familiar with being door-slammed,
Right on the face after being hopeful of the success I had planned
But none of that had me stagnant- I do not mean to blow my own horn,
I am only bringing this to light to remind us all how far each of us has gone
Every journey has a bumpy road, may we never allow hardships deviate
us from the real reasons why we were born,
Every hit you take from life ought to strengthen, not keep you torn
Heal from it all, grow on and allow yourself to become stronger,
Take something from your experiences, that is how you become wiser

Re.Inform & Re.Form

Just an eye opener to the new age historians,
The infants of the conscious community & the knowledge custodians
The intentionally truth-blind that are system bound,
Prisoners of lies that feel comfortable in the propaganda cloud
Our forefathers fought for emancipation, Lincoln did not free them;
Misinformation was given on that proclamation, there was a mayhem
That was began & led by the brave men who dared to stand up,
The men who chose to die on their feet than live on their knees
Who broke the silence & said "Enough! You Do Not Own Us!"
Those are the people we need to be grateful to for taking the
1st step to breeding a generation of born frees

Not the falsified claims where the white man is once again a hero,
That always saves the black house & allegedly elevates it from ground zero
From the 'barbaric' living they accused the natives of leading,
To force-feeding them new customs & religions, among other things
If you are black, I need you to know that you descend from Great Queens & Kings

MEDITATE

For your own peace of mind, you might need to meditate,
Quiet down all mental quarrels & let the soul levitate
No need to medicate, there is a different way to spirit-elevate,
I know how difficult it is to do yourself some good in a world that aggravates
All kinds of adversities, but remember that you are still at liberty,
To turn your life around for the better & ignite your potency
Do it for your own harmony, reconnect with the universe;
Adjust your life to the focus of your destiny, lest you live in reverse
Unlock the chambers on your brain & the secrets of life,
By growing from inside and drawing from within your light
It would be an amazing habit to start doing it every night,
The change may not be instant, but every attempt will up your might
Help with the regain of your concentration & truly change your life
I am certain you are aware of the old saying of a healthy dwelling in a healthy body?
Yea, it goes back to that; this kind of exercise unlocks glory
You get to have inner peace & you retrieve better perspective,
It is like your soul taking over & your mind navigating the drive
Both operating in profound synchrony like nature intended,
Chakras at work ensuring your higher self remains ascended
Enlightenment be intended; Moreover, spiritual transcendence,
I hope you heed my advice, because if you do, prepare to exist in a trance

Go Through Me

To anything tempted, any beast or being threatening my family,
This is an open letter to you, whether or not you are an enemy
In any case, you would be choosing the foe side aiming at my people,
I would not care much about our history, I would rewrite the sequel
Reorder your future at this present moment, this is not a threat,
If you feel I am merely throwing words around – put me to test
No matter the bond we have created, family comes first,
I do not tend to act in emotion but with my day ones I am the worst
& I am aware almost nobody has ever seen me in anguish,
You may enquire my companions when my temper hits me in ambush
There is no telling what the young man would do put in that position,
Body on auto-drive, as if anger is my most diligent passion
I am not saying this in passing, I would fight for anyone behind me,
It has never been about what is in front but what is holding me
The ones on my back, so do believe me when I say I would fight to the bone,
Never held a knife against any throat but I still would not hesitate to reach for the hone
Rip a transgressor to slices with that same knife so he reaps what he has sown,
Better yet, decapitate his head from his limbs, leave his dead self without crown
Put the wrongdoer's merciless death in renown, may his soul depart with a frown,
He better die prepared because in the afterlife, it is second round!

Wise Pick

King, find yourself a cheerleader that will be your quarterback,
One to up your confidence with support, then run to have your back
Better yet, get yourself an open-minded freak that never tests your patience
That will most definitely take care of your soul, not feed it pretence,
The realest of them all, who lives to be your peace & nuisance
Knows her place as a woman, the multiplier of things,
You need her conscious of her being & knowing what her role is
Fully aware of what the potency of her mind potentially brings,
Imagine finding a strong-spirited woman, would that not be pure bliss?
So please! If you yearn for good health & wealth, you need to do this
You must stay sane for anything you are trying to achieve to succeed,
A prosperous man tends to be well-rooted by a great queen
A kind lady that never allows her emotions to cloud her judgement,
Yes, she may be compassionate, but that must never compromise her advancement
She has to see things like you do or you will seldom be in agreement,
& every time you try to talk it out, there will first be an argument
And somewhere deeper in marriage, things will feel worse,
1st it will be taking a little break from each other; then next will be divorce
So, do not set yourself up for failure, make choices of certainty,
Ensure she is the love of your life & that you adore her completely

The Big Small Talk

I feel like a black sheep that views the world differently,
Like sighting on an upside perspective with nobody to notice me
Or if they do, they hardly ever comprehend the real Athel,
& most times it feels like heaven, some days it is just hell
That is how I prefer it, frankly... but if you need reasons, I will tell –
Seeing things your own way gives you an urge of self-confidence,
It supports the dogma that says, within us dwells splendid providence
This might sound crazy & naïve, but do also think from inside of your cage,
Curious & crazy minds always seem to have influence in change
Take the highest leap of faith in your abilities & your power,
Allow your self-esteem to steam up aloft, higher than any tower
But still remain humble – we need confidence & not ego,
One is knowing you are capable, the other strongly believes
things take his path when they go
That is acting G.O.D, man know yourself & what you can control,
Also, what you cannot, to avoid self-pity & blame when things take toll
& remember, life is nothing but an experience of your mind,
Take that knowledge & always know you must seek it within first before
you can really find
You are the driver of your own destiny, that is how I hope all this sounds

Unanswered Questions

There are days that make me feel dead inside,
Days when hope feels like nothing but a waste of time
When you do not even know who plays the drums to your silly song,
Is it G.O.D, ancestors or just the universe making it all go wrong?
How pleased is the event-setter at your very moment of break down?
When you cry your eyes to sore & swell, are they smiling to the fall of your crown?
Yea, I know how it all sounds… but I really do wish to know
Is whoever writing our storylines amused by how bad things go?
Are we just impromptu actors they sit in their chambers to watch?
And when we go through the worst, all they can do is wish we could be in touch,
So they can intervene from heavenly paradise, high up in the skies?
Is the higher power sometimes so powerless to rescue humanity when it dies?
Are we all just fooling our minds when we look for miracles,
Praying for at least a sign, since there is never a reply to our cries?
These are questions that surface when you feel life-ridiculed,
But they forever remain unanswered; until birds, mites & dust turns us into food

Heart To Heart

Addictions are the worst things, you need to be careful,
Let me tell you a little story, so you do not act like a fool
I know a young man who is so addicted to pleasure,
And on top of all that, he is an adrenaline junky
So, he tends to act certain ways just to feed those urges in his leisure,
& when I say certain ways, I assure you that those ways are nothing close to good or even better
After every wrongdoing he almost gets caught... stupid dummy,
So, tell me this as man dying; do not play either you or me
How many chances do you think fate gives to transgressors?
& won't every successful attempt bring karma even closer?
Do you really want to risk all you have got for a puny habit?
Listen, if it is a hazard to your future, you best lay back off it,
Here, take a sip of some heart to heat; Get your life in order before you regret it

Sthembiso Ayanda Shabalala

Salient

It is either a blessing or a curse, you choose what to make of it,
Whether you took it as a lesson or a straight up failure, you decide what you take from it
Your trials & tribulations are to you what you make them,
Is it a fair chance of growth or a complete mayhem?
Your perspective is inception of all you have before you,
It begins as a thought & manifests through the tongue or deed
I know I have no idea what each of us is going through,
But I can promise you peace of mind if you listen & take heed
You carry a powerful tool with every waking day & night
& you seem to ignorant to that fact, or does it give you a fright?
You bear a key to all doors & that is a point to take home,
The answer to all your questions resides high up in your dome
So, it would be in your best interest to ensure viability of your sanity,
But whatever you do, do not be chained by your own reality
Remember all you see, smell, touch or hear is what your brain makes,
So, in simpler terms... it is in your disposal to influence
what shape your present moment takes
Keep thinking your own thoughts, do not forget about the invisible,
Because you cannot see a force, it does not mean it is not viable
What is perceived by the conscious mind may be viewable,
But the unconscious is what renders everything tangible pliable

Drive Tease

Baby, can we take a drive a little sedated & drive naked?
With you laying on my chest, let all emotions awaken
Clear all smokes in our life & strip our souls bear to each other,
In fact, I need us to get really deep within one another
& if the other person does not reach base of pit, we advance further,
You know you are a book I placed in my heart's shelves at first eye glance,
A deck of cards I only want to shuffle without play chance
Yea I am being honest, the King is not playing joker,
You best be ready to ride the game of hearts with me forever
I love reading your character, but I hope you are not running script,
I hope this is all real because you make something inside of me skip
& trust me, I hate omissions, but it is out of mind's control;
You are all to blame, my commission to you has me vulnerable
It is something like a hypnotic effect, the most compelling call,
Every time I am with you, I tend to feel invincible
So unpredictable, I become so versatile & spontaneous,
It is very glorious, just me & you my baby, with nobody disturbing us
I am serious... allow us to take a ride for the night, that is what I want,
This is something we never did; can we go experiment?
Make memories with you because I never want to forget you,
Even if we end breaking up, my mind would not bear to lose you
The lot of things that we have & are still going to go through,
Are always drawing closer & I know they strengthen us too
So, let us use this moment to create a stronger bond in a crazy way,
Please, say yes & allow our love to survive for more other days

Sthembiso Ayanda Shabalala

My Letter Of Affection

My pillar of strength, do not turn on what we have,
You are the only peace I have left in this world till the grave
I know I am being blue, but I must rephrase in case you have forgotten,
You are the only factor needed to keep my world alight to infinity
Affection as airborne as an infection like my love was ill-gotten,
When it is a condition of loyalty that know no life's fidelity
I would love to keep it that way just as long as Universe wills
Those are the vibes I fully attract with my head over heels,
Moments of thrill, you are the fantasy that feels real
Dream that I live, a wish the man has been granted,
Under a night full of stars with neither aligned
Where silly promises were made & seeds of joy planted,
Blowing clouds to the sky, appreciating how our living was designed
May out mental lobes that connect never resign, may they never die;
Should the breathing ability escape our lungs, let all feelings ascend fly
To dimensions that will embrace & sustain us through eternity,
Validating our interweave, ensuring you are never dodging me
I find true satisfaction in just holding your hand & caring for you,
So do get this: every time I am around it feels right to be by you

Love & War

Since the world is against us, then I guess it is me & you against it,
They have been judging & verbally stoning at us & I truthfully hate that
So, from now on it is just the two of us, disregard the intrusions,
Because they see nothing wrong with what they are doing – making up conclusions
No idea how we met or even how we got to this point in our love,
How you were on a deathbed the 1st time we began our love life
A simple social media text turned into a blessing from above,
I know it never made sense how I fell for you, why you for my affection?
You do not need to reply to that, it is a rhetorical question
The direction you took when I was approaching you had my attention,
I was just a stranger helping another, nothing much to it,
But as we spoke more, I knew I had to sweep you off your feet
Each day we conversated felt like I was just talking to myself,
You were all me, everything you said was what I would also say myself
Like the universe moulded your spark just for me & had the stars align,
But now the ones under the sky have a dilemma with you being mine
All the haters do not approve, toleraters are moved by jealousy,
And the rest of the people around us are dying of envy
I say let us put them out of their miseries, you do not even have to look,
Arm yourself and come with me; close your eyes, imagine
us in our room & then start kissing me
If it means fighting for us to survive then I guess it is time to choose,
Tell me, are you willing to go to war for us even though we might lose?

Sthembiso Ayanda Shabalala

IAmKing

I do not follow orders, do not mistaken me for a sheep
Yea, for now I may be cheap but pretty soon I will reap,
My sows will show progress & all these doubters will weep
I wear caps as crowns, my head is never open,
Yet I think out of the box like my imagination resides in a brain that is wide open
You can call me an open-closed book, only if that is where you are heading,
But to remain bold, humble & winning is what I am always aiming
& try my best to be a shepherd who walks before his flock,
Leading by example & never paying attention to any deposited talk
Recall my day ones at the bottom as soon as I reach the top,
Give them lessons of being generous, tell them greediness must stop
I have always known my place, this is why I move in my own pace,
Do you think I want glow? Please look at my face
I want nothing but glory, that has always been my chase,
Be a King in his own write, number 1 on the pen race
Why is royalty hated when it is self-proclaimed, I am asking?
If you are who you believe to be, then I Am King!

The Boy

Let me tell you a little story of a boy born of nothing yet still yearns for glory
Owning nothing but a mind full of words,
Emotions shake them out & put the pen to work
A broken broke writer without a dime to his name,
Who has a financial beast within him that nobody can ever tame
With all he has lost, the boy grows grateful for what he has left,
Smiling & caring with a heart engraved by wounds that cleft
Self-proclaimed King with a slightly humongous ego,
Questioning everything around him for he is too eager
With each complete peace of writing, his confidence grows bigger,
The boy knows the ground too well, thus he always fights to be & remain a winner
This lad had to learn how to care for himself at a very young age
The lack of biological parents put his heart in a cage,
But that is a story for a different day, for now let us close this page

Sthembiso Ayanda Shabalala

Vent

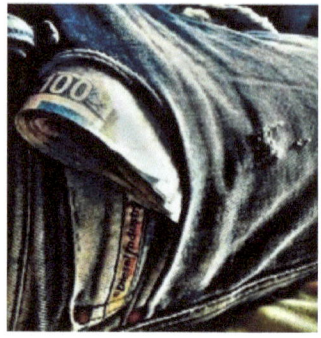

To tell the truth, I do not find any woman a turner any more,
Most of them are ungrateful, you give them one thing & they want more
You give her the ocean of love, she makes demands for the shore,
My walled oasis of affection has been done away with, it is only left with pores
A major number of females are soul killers & believe me you, I have a strong desire to live;
Material things will most probably be slight healers, even though
I do not mean to seem like I have no care to give
Frankly, I do… but tell me, how can you feel entitled to a person
when you cannot own you?
If you do not love your own self, who is meant to love you?
If you do not make a win for the bread, who is expected to feed you?
So my focus is truly shifted & it makes me feel gifted,
Even on dark days, my ambition remains well-lifted
I do not even own a driver's license, yet I stay driven;
I am goal conscious – I aspire to be wealthy… we all know
that is a given, there is really nothing hidden
I woke up with the same paper depression as I did yesterday, I detest this type of living,
Writing it is therapeutic to me, do please read when I am venting!

The Growth Show

I grew up boosting me own spirit. Telling myself I am capable as long as I put my mind to it,
Telling self failure will never put me down, instead I must learn from it
I grew up patting my own shoulder, upping my own confidence, motivating my own self,
Like, "it is a long road to success, do not mind what comes with the distance!"
I grew up looking up to nobody but my past mistakes,
That is why my spirit will never break
Not by anybody nor by anything and I am never fake,
I am a seed, even if you burry me I will always surface up. I cause my own fate!
Damn! I am actually angry at G.O.D
I have been loyal to prayer, I always speak to the lord,
But what happened on this day broke me up like rod
I cannot really cry about it, it will only make me stronger,
I take any adversity as a lesson & that keeps me a winner
I did not plan on writing this but I had to blow steam
What I went through today almost stole away my dream,
But I will never give in & trust me, that I mean!

Sthembiso Ayanda Shabalala

No Saint Nor Sinner

I am a villain to someone's story, does that make me evil?
I admit to have been a culprit of inflicting some kind of pain
Yes, I am not really perfect, but do we know such as people?
The only flawlessness we know is the one locked inside our brains,
& no matter how good looking or behaving, the truth remains
Good & bad hold equal reign within us, we choose which one thrives,
The decisions we take each day decide which force governs our lives
If the powers that be allowed us the liberty to pick our ways,
Then our autonomy is what moulds our characters every night & day
& every deed or utter is always a confession of that very moment's dominant side,
Stop looking for strength outside – inside is where your glory resides
It never even hides, you just ought to realise your true capabilities
If whoever you kneel to only helps those who help themselves,
Then why belittle the ability to offer yourself that help?
Life is a set of choices made according to our perceptions,
Free will need not turn into ill-will, be your own redemptions
Whether you yield light or darkness, that will be your own decision,
Heaven & hell are a state of mind… that is my own conclusion

My Centrepiece

You wanted to know what gives me peace? Having you in my arms,
No matter how emotional or frustrated, it always keeps me calm
In essence, you are the remedy I need to keep my demons on leash,
And I thank the universe every waking day for granting my wish
If it were not for you, I would probably be a junky if not a suicidee;
You gave me a different life perspective that truly saved me
Now I realise that life is what you make it, we only win if we want to,
Circumstances may come unforeseen, but we choose whether to remain or push through
You are my place of better thoughts, my escape from the cold world,
Even though we fight like cat & dog, I hope together we grow old
Rather have that with you than someone else – for better or worse,
Till death do our flesh part, you are my blessing & my curse
& I know in the afterlife our souls will stay intertwined,
When our offspring kneel to a deity of ancestors, it should be us
That is how far my vision stretches about us; with all well-aligned,
I have sought but could not find the right one to fully blow my mind
Just as you availed my view about love was forever changed,
What I have become since our encounter feels more familiar than strange
I guess you helped discover my true self without destroying the old,
Helped me evolve to a greater being without having my story fold
You turned a peasant into a King by simply agreeing to be his Queen,
That is why I hold you very tight & close to my heart beat
You are like nothing I have ever had – a creation I have never seen
My angel, you are the centrepiece of my unrooted feet,
I never want to go a night without you, I need you in my cold sheets

Bulb Burst

I have been having sleepless nights lately, tossing & turning,
Ideas flowing in & out of my brain, my priorities are burning
Bouncing ideas on self & the drawing board, praying they never go south,
I try keeping them contained but you know the human mouth
It hardly stops running when great thoughts are on track,
Especially when those thoughts are in line with getting stacks
I wake up every morning & work on my sketched plans,
The blueprint of the whole future construct on my humble hands
It is time for everything locked inside of the light bulb to be set free
For every little good thought enclosed to manifest into reality,
And all actions to mimic the imaginary, even if it is scary
Growth can be very overwhelming & giving in can be so tempting,
Shake off that failure temptation, you have plenty of options
There are plenty of other ways to get to your accomplishments,
Ensure your self-morale on high mode & allow inflow of innovation
Think deep about your plans & execute towards your advancement,
You will do yourself some justice, let us have that agreement?

In-Borne Terror

I am already cruel to myself, I do not need anyone else to be;
I have judged myself already, I do not need you to judge me
Do not think of killing me, I already think of suicide every day I am awake;
I am not asking for the world's demons, I have my own I cannot seem to shake
Pain I am unable to take away; a sorrow I can never cry nor wipe away,
I moan a deathless mourn but still I remain an unrecognizable stray
Everybody around notices my silence, yet my tragedy is unseen;
A million virtual friends, not even one asks how I have been
The voices in my head are getting scarier & louder!
I have no way to mute them up, herbs are not helping either,
Living is getting harder, with every sunset & sunrise I grow bitter
Slowly adapting to the darkness, all terrors gone terrific
All my phobias on play; from claustrophobia alone, climbing to being photophobic,
I have gotten used to living in the deepest shades of self-pity & guilt,
For things I have never felt adequate for, so I have set myself to quit
What I mean is, I wear an invisible noose as a tie around my neck all of my days
Self-sabotage to its highest form while everyone is living on,
They are entertained by the façade, a decoy from my true face
I am a voiceless miserable soul crying out for help to show on,
Would you stop ignoring the clear signs & start putting your care on?

Sthembiso Ayanda Shabalala

Unheard Cries

They do not understand the agony of a stab until the knife flips to cut them,
They never really feel pain until the tables start to turn
All these victims just want attention when they run to speak to them,
Worst yet, they just want to pull a publicity stunt plan
Whenever victims try to speak out, real snakes begin to come out,
But as soon as fate knocks at the snakes' door, they are scared to go out
To face their own woes in the eyes of their foes,
When such waters flood their own homes & get them tipping toes
That is when they really begin to get it; fog off every disregardful eye,
In that very moment is when they begin to see it, the person told no lie
The day they realise it will be way too late, the damage will be done
Culprits will have made more damage in the world with no remorse shown,
& the sexually, emotionally or physically offended might be gone
Some spiritually and other gone mentally – no longer in sober minds,
Sedating every chance they can get, maybe trying to fill holes
That screw with sound thoughts as they hope they can unwind,
A problem eventually adds to another, addiction now makes them whole
All because they were made afraid to open up about this adversity
Let us be less ignorant, help create a less damaged future society,
The offended ought to be given the benefit of the doubt when telling their story

All In A Jar

I can give you the universe in a jar, I swear I can make you a star,
Since I have never met your kind on this earth, you are a Goddess by far
A glory flower to my eyes, a tree of life to the vast majority,
I am telling no lies, feel free to call bluff on frank me
I bless the day I laid sight on you, my beautiful mermaid
& I pinkie promise that my affection for you is not man-made
No, it is not artificial… if anything, it is way too natural,
Can you not see me handing you my whole self on a palm?
And you know too well I have never intentionally did you foul,
I have given you the crown & always acted out that balm
My words in regard to you; efforts given to you in proof,
Life of an introvert given to you straight on a hand's loof
Do not drop it, it is fragile… please handle with care,
It has been messed with one too many times, do not induce any tear
You can give me that blank stare but I am dead serious,
I am very much cautious – love tends to make me delirious
If you must know, I trust you with myself for I believe in us,
Yea, I believe in you and all that you stand for – I truly am for us
So long as you play your part in ensuring you do not break us apart,
I am more than pleased & honoured to let you take care of my heart

Cloud 9

When reality feels too unbearable, I run to hide in the 9th cloud,
Isolate for a while & let all the voices in my head get loud
It is like a board meeting... discussing our future, present & past,
Seventh heaven replicas of council within a King, so steadfast
Every bright day, communicating to retain sanity & levity,
To keep the shoulders of the physical being from opposing gravity
Head above the dirty toxic water contaminated by life's evils,
To a self-created atmosphere that keeps out minds that are feeble
This is my kind of meditation; a practise crucial peace & focus
Being by myself and allow my thoughts to wander without fuss,
Dwell in a quiet state where no disturbance can make me cuss
Or else run to lock myself in a room buzzing with sound,
And start creating phrases out of words that my mind has found
Just to help keep out the ones who have never reached this end,
Raise an awareness of what that kind of living is for every friend
It does nothing but life-sucks & sends you to an early grave,
Even though some of us have made it to the side adaptation
That kind of existing requires a strong mind and a will that is brave
But however profound it gets, I know escaping is an option,
If you are on this side of the fence, know skipping can be a decision

Anati's Life Lesson

I know a little girl, now a woman, who grew up as an orphan,
Had nobody to advocate for her fairness, so she was sent often
Under a hand of a cruel aunt, in her grandmother's crib,
Her kids would be given special treatment, Anati would frequently get whipped
Just for starting chores late – she would receive a rod to her rib,
But if the favourites opt to have them undone, they are helped
They are not even scolded to do them, they are just left
Anati frequently wondered if anybody understood how she felt
Why she was put in a family that only views her as their maid,
Not as a child needing care & guidance – that made her very mad
Most times when she is sad, she would just grab her phone & freely vent,
That is how she became a writer, writing to erase anybody's dent
To change and touch a lot of lives with only the issue of her words,
Sang unmelodious heal songs to all the wandering broken birds
A compass to the lost even though life has been nothing but harsh,
Even when her only crime was losing her parents on that car crash
She still stood for what she believed in; never allowed herself to get bitter,
Learnt the best out of that adversity, the past no longer matters
What is important is making sure she is getting better,
While she proceeds on focusing on climbing her self-constructed ladder
Moral of the story? Take the best lessons out of your hardships,
And whatever happens, do not let them turn you into a trip

SuperComputer

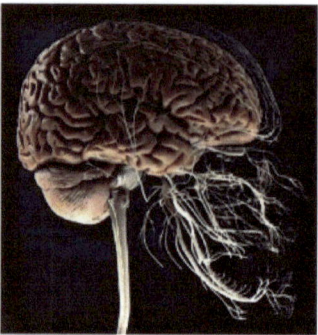

All that you are is just your mind at work,
All that you believe in is what makes sense to your brain's logic
& every movement you make is your conscious self sending orders,
That move up & down your nerves via multi-synaptic borders
Acetylcholine & Dopamine being the driving neurotransmitters,
Even better, every time you make it through time, you grow wiser
Because your memory bank deposits every little experience,
Puts every moment on record; such pays you with expedience
Making it suitable for you to evolve & survive, it is how you stay alive,
We are living in a jungle, only the fittest can thrive
But that declares no war nor competition amongst human kind,
All that it means is, to remain afloat you need to retain a smarter mind
But in any case... allow me not to unintentionally digress,
Knowing who & what you are is what I am trying to address
You are a monumental Super-Computer – you need to realise,
The only difference between you & the artificial one is that your reality is not virtualized
& that the one you are is the one that created the other one,
If you were a weapon of any calibre, you would be an aboriginal gun
Lock and load all your energy on that magazine – the war has begun,
Take note of your nature & put it to proper use before you are gone!

Eligible Affection

We read each other like books, we care not how it looks
Everyday is the same study day, Friday is no different from a Sunday
To read each other like a bible, as the word says
It is more like your religions, except this one is of love,
We believe in each other so much, there is no one else above
Novels of reality admixed with fantasy in the chambers of memory,
Sects of history & what is to be like scripts of theology
Yet so profane in analogy, all engraved on you & me
Every pleasure & pain written on us; passion oozing out of skin pores,
This is bigger than our comprehension, we divinely are one
Too much that there is no sense of sanity without the other,
I just hope you are in this for sure, do not sign up to be gone
My pages are not for play or tear – do not mend me just to have me torn,
For you, I believe I was solely born; stop my doubts from living on
With that pen of affection you hold on your hand, write what is right;
& remember every action or word made known to me brings the ink to light to write
I give you the power to rewrite my insecurities, I beg for justice
Shade all the wrongs scribbled on my soul and please offer me peace?

Sthembiso Ayanda Shabalala

Literal Read

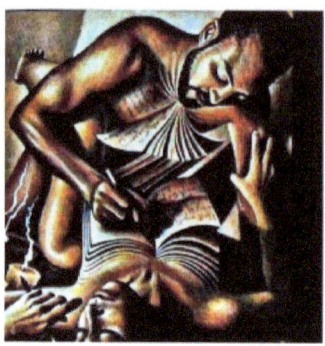

Do not look at me with quick glance, get deeper like a book;
Read me from my physique to my mind, all the way into my soul
You might need plenty of intelligence and time – I am a piece of work,
& you will need to invest some kind of energy too or I will be a haul
I will truly be heavy to bear with, like a very heavy load to carry,
And whatever trait I give off, I will strike you off as scary
Do me as I ask because I will be doing you just as I expect,
I do not advertise my persona, I suppose you have to be an analyst
I am not an easy read, I might be perceived as uninterestingly boring
Those who do not comprehend my character would find me annoying
Utterly confusing, like a wordsmith hell-bound by dyslexia,
Or a grown man in a comma living through a period of amnesia
So I stopped trying to make the scars imprinted up my sleeves,
Become relevant to anybody attempting to come into my life and leave
Instead, I let the monster inside of me live his life of pleasure,
Until I found a lady that was willing to read me even on leisure
Everything felt better, I found myself lost in her brood all the time,
I would find myself lost in the feel of it all, I swear that girl is a dime
We keep an open feed of everything – no secrets inside of our love,
Moreover, I am into the fact that she knows where to press
to make my senses groove, sleek moves!

What About Your Dreams?

May we soon begin to be a self-considerate generation,
Because these days, that is one of many things it takes to preserve a nation
I mean, every race is acting wise about what they put their monies on,
While our own black house is senseless, like they have no idea what is going on
What is really going on? Why is everyone around me pretentiously acting blind?
Like they are unable to uncover the keys they have always sought to find?
Like they have no clue that the future they are trying to
build rests solely on their own hands?
That the bright life everyone is hoping to attain depends on each of our plans!
& I do not mean just thinking or verbalising your scheming,
I am speaking of planning to execute & following out your ideas
May I not be misunderstood; I am not playing favourites, but everyone
seems to be woke except my siblings,
The lot that becomes stuck even with a piece of paper to attest to their years
Behind a desk serving time they were never even asked permission to give,
We were all just born & handed human-constructed guides on how we should live
But in that life laid out for us, we are still shooting in the dark,
Rephrasing the lessons our parents & the society instilled in us like
one about success being defined as looking fancy
Or frequent night outs with friends to have unbudgeted drinks,
While other ethnic groups are pacing up daily better than a vast majority
of us to make money
We are out drinking it off or purchasing flaunt-worthy luxury,
Take time to think of it; is that what making it truly is?
Are we that desperate to add value to our poor selves that we miss
what the actual meaning of making it means?

Façade Off

I had to think of ways I can utilize to make them understand me,
But none of these masks I have worn have truly helped me
All they did was attract more misconception & loss of self,
I had gotten used to the dress up, almost ended up forgetting about the real Athel
I would often wonder who I am when in my dome, sitting in lone,
Especially after inhaling burnt trees... like am I still the person I have always known?
Am I on a transition of becoming a man – is the boy in me now gone?
Is this what my circumstances have made or it is just the old me grown?
Questions of this calibre have made me feel unbelonging... worst yet, unworthy
Undeserving of any kind of affection & care anyone around tried to give me,
I mean I failed to offer that affect to me, why should anyone else?
If I cannot take care of myself, how could I have expected the next one to care?
Why starve this much to have external love while internally it is not there?
No love nor appreciation given to who I am until I began to realise,
That I must begin to work on my self-borne curse
Accept my actual being & love dearly the man I am becoming,
Thus, the fact that I got myself more than anyone else should never be shocking
I have cared about people's approval longer than it should have endured
Neglected me, who I wanted to be & what I want to be in accord,
Self-defraud! The rest put themselves first & their own blood
But through retrospect I made an introspection & set my priorities straight,
I now know what I want & anything that goes against that, I will not tolerate!

Guilty As Charged

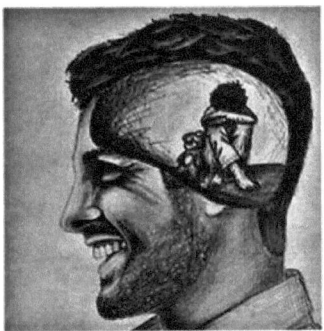

I admit it, I am a mess... I act all tough, but it is bad;
I know I seem fine with life as it stands, but deep down I am sad
Even worse – I carry around childhood nightmares & terrors,
Not your typical grim reaper, feared hideous mammal or murder case kind of horror
I mean the real-life people wrong you & break,
To a point of beyond repairs; funny thing is, they almost always never see any mistake
They hardly realise the damaged they had previously caused – what was at stake,
Living on like there is not a piece of sanity they most likely take
I am also one of the victims of disappointment and pain,
My silence does not mean I am guilty of those crimes or if I want to be put through the same past again
In fact, the past is what turns me into a mute just as feelings avail,
It forces me to think of how I have put my buttocks on the line for petty girls
And mentally takes me back to a lonely dark room when I was a kid,
Sobbing about why I never deserved a biological parent to keep me hid
One to fight my wars, clear my woes & some days do my chores,
It is in those days that some sort of revelation about me hit my door
That maybe I was never meant for nurturing love, but tough one goes
I guess I psychologically learnt how to be that like tracks on the floor,
So, take me as I am; help me grow & adore me forever more

To My Forever

The sweet nothings you whispered in my ears give me vivid dreams
When you hissed that vocal melody of life & utter security,
I cringed from goosebumps on my skin for a second, literally
You told me you got me all the way & you will love me forever
Yes, I am bringing that up, did you think I would not remember?
I told you I will hold you to it, that you truly mean it;
And that you should never say something if you do not mean it
But in your case, I feel like you meant every single word you stuttered,
With your voice shaking from thinking how much you love this bastard
Yet that never stopped you from moving your mouth down my neck,
Caressing my head in finesse like you are about to ride me on the desk
When all I ask? Be with me everyday & respect me in every way
Do not allow me to stop you though – go on & play with me however way you want,
I foresee a whole life with you; do your will, I am yours either way
Proceed scratching on my body without leaving a dent,
I always die to have you for dinner, now being smoke-clear blunt
Just the thought of ripping that shirt off alone gives me chills
& you know very well how it feels – it gives us both a thrill,
But then again, off intimate talk & straight back to what I want for real
To give you the world on platinum platter for every day you are with me
For all the love & time you hand to me… most of all for caring for me,
There is nobody I would rather share with my eternity, honestly

Hometown Taylor

I told them, "give me a canvas & I will mend your hearts",
I will write down some remedy to make you feel alright
Scribble for you a few lines of healing in the form of art,
Something to gently rub on your soul every day & night
Allow me to get you through therapy, I will only do it verbally;
Physically you may not feel a thing but spiritually you will definitely feel me
I will be tapping into realms nobody is ever allowed to reach,
With a verse without prayer, no I do not really preach
I am just like your oldest hometown tailor,
Fixing the broken & being their voice while I make them feel better
I give myself plenty of time to make a proper sewing,
& most of my lads wonder how I do what I am doing
It is quite easy… I merely allow the mind to express how it feels,
Let it construct multiple syllables to inform about its good times & its ills
It actually does not matter how I do it,
All that matters is that you find consolation & peace when you read through it
So do yourself some justice & give up your broken self for a mend,
I promise you it is pain free & whenever I touch you, misery ends

Sthembiso Ayanda Shabalala

Hate

These days I have been busy minding my own,
May I never have any kind of emotion towards anything that is not mine,
Keep shooting for the win & embrace how I have grown,
I mean, in the end that is all it takes to retain sanity in your mind
"Are you led by your spirit or your past wounds?"
I am pretty sure most of us it is just wounds,
Mind you! I said most of US it is just wounds!
Me inclusive; pain has ruined me & has made me feel indecisive,
Became so closed up & got angry at anybody invasive
Not only that, I can no longer trust any of you humans
I am capable of more love, but I drop an inch to remain humane,
You tend to bite the hand that feeds you – yes, I am looking at you, man!
You are a fan to my face & run to rumour behind my back,
Then you run to my place just as karma fires back to plead to be accepted back?
No, I think this I will pass… I needed you back then,
Hypocrisy left you at zero point none & life placed me at ten

To Whom It May Concern

I think you are quarrelling with me, even though it is on low
And the punch is indirect, that is sadly a low blow,
I hope you know where to run to for your due sorrows
Because I am a hazard, I even put my reputation on my logo
So that each time you see me you are reminded that I am a zone of no go,
I stretched out my hands every time you fell, so
I had to learn the hardest way that there is a Judas in every crew,
The funny & hurtful part is that you were the only crew
I had in this city, only one to turn to
But we do choose our own ways, what can I honestly do?
You chose to run against me, what a darn fool!
You are nothing but a confused smoke trying to oppose a tragically strong wind,
I guess you will only get to understand that as soon as I make meet with my ends
We live in a life of tables & pretty soon they will begin to turn
For now, you may be standing on tall trees, they will soon start to burn,
I dive hard for my keep, that is why I will keep goaling all my plans
I wrote this letter to you, anonymous,
The growth with or without you will still be enormous
You thought my plane will crash without you, well at least that is what you could discern,
This is an open letter, To Whom It May Concern

Dear Self

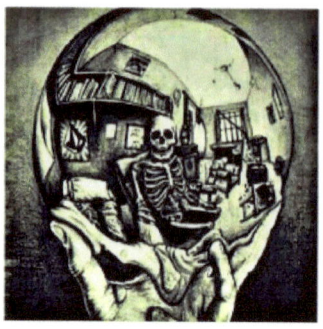

Within you lies tremendous potential you need to unleash,
You are a river of greatness – you need flow relentless if you are to reach
Do not take whatever they say, man; be the best you,
Just like anybody else, you have vision too
See things your own way, not their way... Ray Charles to their bogus ways
People will always talk, some will even hate,
Some will share a rate but others will emulate
Create your destiny & give no chance to fate,
Work towards your prime, young man; it is never too late
I know lately you have been feeling like there is no point to anything at all,
Making your motions without emotion to keep intact & never hurt at all
Applying your confidence like lotion, mind remaining deeper than the ocean,
Reading & replying to texts with remorseless notions
'Never lose yourself, trying to be held'
Do you still recall when you thought of that quote you were in hell?
When silence was the loudest scream, louder than any bell?
With no one to share your woes with, nobody to ever tell?
You have always recalled your lessons & every reason you fell,
Preserving your honesty, despite all the lies they tell
Realise your worth & never settle for less
You will indefinitely keep winning as long as you stay humble & remember that you are blessed,
Dear self... never give strength to any weakness

Revenge

Before embarking on a journey of revenge – dig two graves,
Such pursuits require hatred & hate can consume us
Revenge may be calculated but it treats us like slaves,
Because we lose ourselves in the process & we are never truly us
We become the dead living, revenge has no healing,
Holding on to the past assists not with pain dealing
It only keeps the scars open, hinders them from sealing up like they are ought to be,
So, whatever you do… let bygones be & live your life being free
In order to live an existence without burdens – forgive all wrongs,
Even if it means talking, writing or singing about it in songs
Just do what you must to move on,
Live with a sound mind with no conflicting voices screaming on
I wrote under this picture to paint a death image,
To put you in the frame of what can occur when you react to rage
There is no freedom with such mentality, it keeps you in a cage,
And while your peers enjoy life, you quickly age

Music All Along

Ask me what life would be without music?
Ask if I'd be where I am if my hero was not symphonic?
So I can tell you all about my dark days,
When I could not never share with anybody my worst strays
Tell you about how I have had to carry dead weight on my shoulder,
Face the music of my own making & take responsibility because I am older
Ask me now so I can let the pen shed tears,
Scribble my pain for you, perhaps I can prevent psychological snares
That may lead down to the road of emotional fears,
Allow me to share it now even though no one cares
Music has had my back since day one,
Carried me from pain to joy via tv, radio or a phone
Have you never wondered why it is a craft I one day want to carve too?
I want to create it and help someone get through anything too
From a frown, straight face and all the way up to a smile,
The effect it can be able to go is more than a mile
When all has gone wrong songs can be remedial,
So let them correct the wrong that is inside...

Insecure You

Baby, I will need you to bear with me,
I swear I am real with you but I am new to monogamy
You know all about my past & where I have been,
Who I have been with before & who I have seen
We have spoken about this; I told what I am about,
Tell me lover, have I given you reasons for any doubt?
Then why are your insecurities when it comes me this loud?
Have I not shown my friends & family that you are in my life, told them I am proud?
So let us sit down & talk, what is with all this commotion?
Are you with me because you can or to put our love in motion?
You never answered any of my questions, am I a fool now?
Why am I talking alone like you are a bull now?
I am truly getting fed up of explaining my every move,
Each time I sneeze, I must give you reasons of why I have flue?
Tell me, is this a hell hole prison or place of love?
Was it a crime that I fell for you? Was I the one who broke you?
I have been transparent with you but your trust issues are blocking the view,
You are too blind to the beauty of all the hues...

Hand A Heart?

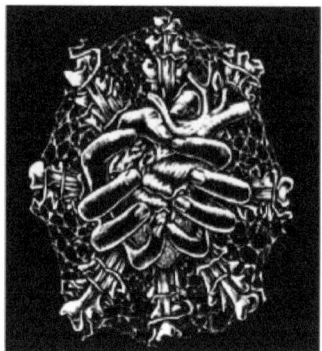

People find heaven in taking but hell in giving,
They find joy in receiving instead of sharing love
The reason there are wounds that go without healing,
Is because handing forgiveness is harder than asking it from above
We expect abundant inflow but withhold any outflow
That is why generosity feels like strapping your head on a death rope,
Why good people in our lives yearn to put us in a list of outgrows
We kill pure hearts, feed them wrath & dead hopes,
Then good souls die, leaving live bodies feeling as corpses
No good deed goes unpunished? Then all good folks must perish,
And do believe me, these words are written in anguish
I am a victim of good doing that always results into a furnace,
Burning all existing affection, dropping my caring heart to menace
I could hand you a heart but you will only find it fit for harness,
And in the end, I will be left with regrets of allowing you to improve while I digress

Is He Jailed?

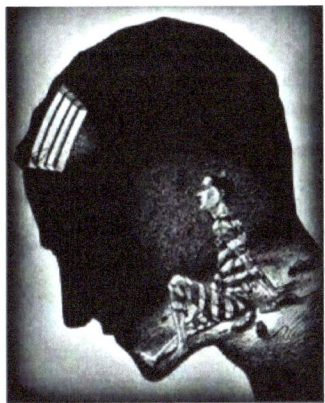

Good lord, I am feeling under pressure!
I have been scheming & plotting daily, there is no time for leisure
It is like I am locked in my own head like a cell,
I am not in sound mind yet it is frustratingly noisy in my head
I cannot even hear my own thoughts like my neurons hit a bell,
I think this & think of that, from my brain ideas shed
Moreover, lately I have been hitting my head for mere expression,
I have no idea of what is going on, it is like inner me took a vacation
Like the actual author inside of me has turned mute on me,
Or the black brother is locked up & has no resources to reach me
It seems the situation within is hostile,
Because the speaker in my mind is no longer in docile
Must improvise to get me back these words?
Do I need inspiration, herbs or a few medications for the lad?
Or I need a little talk with myself to have peace?
What am I to do? May I get ideas, please?

Sthembiso Ayanda Shabalala

Who Have I On My Back?

These days it is hard to see if people have my back or not,
I do not know if they want what is best for me or what
Whether they see a lost course or just a puppet to push around;
A man with tremendous potential or just a piñata to pound
I keep getting calls from the world I have tried ample times to disconnect,
From the people who almost killed my soul & saw me as nothing but a reject
The very same people who doubted I would ever make it,
When I saw something in myself & attempted to bless it to illuminate
my future, they only tried to curse it
Water under the bridge though, the pen to write my days was never in their hands,
The only One I look up & beg is the man on the mirror, only he knows my life plans
With everything considered, I am verily glad I tripped;
Or I would have never known who is genuinely with me and who has flipped
I would be out here hitting people up for favours,
For that reason, I am happy that I stood back & took notes of all behaviours
In doing that, I stumbled upon profound revelations,
This is why I am this certain I want to cut particular connections

Adversaries

Man, I feel like death, yet I inhale & exhale;
My updates of social media may give you a glimpse of my tale
I never really confide, you can call it pride,
But logs of traps by my enemies are not what I wish to ride
I keep steady even with everything shaking,
I smile through misery even when my heart is aching
I have no game plan this time around, to speak in truth,
I am doing my complete best to keep it together but nothing seems to be good
These are nothing close to complaints, I merely venting on my pad,
The canvas is my shrink, it allows me to be the bigger man whenever I need to blow steam or feel sad
And to whoever I have been rude, I am facing mental feud,
Accept my apologies for all that – it is this incident that exposes my crude
I am a man who seldom deals well with fall,
But whenever I hit the ground, I find ways to crawl
I will soon surface up; the ground was never my place,
And I will proceed attracting vibes, ensuring the frequency matches my preferred growing pace
What I am currently going through will prepare me for what I am about to head to,
Whatever is at hand will put me down and raise me up too

Sthembiso Ayanda Shabalala

The Grim Visits

I have been having constant visits from the grim,
Each time I close my eyes, I see him
Standing there with 2 shinning objects seeming as blades on each of his hands
Staring at my face, most probably thinking I will shiver in his glance
What in the 7 hells is this, for heaven's sake!?
Is it a sign that I am the one he is here to take?
Is this where it all stops, where my journey ends?
Or he is just here to visit cold me & make a request of being friends?
Because he is always just there in blank stare,
Why is he not making a move? Perhaps he is well aware I have no fear
Whether I live or die, whether he takes me or leaves me there, I do not really care;
I am not afraid of this monster, he is not fit to be my nightmare
He clearly came to me without being given a memo,
The intrepidness I bear is my little secret armour
It would be therefore best for him to go before I confront him & let him know,
Instead of him scaring me, I am intrigued by how bright his blades glow
He is having a hard time deciding whether to take me, obviously
If he could, he would have done it already
Before I saw him in my dreams and/or day visions several times,
Before I put the puzzle together, put it all in line
Letting the cat out of the bag... this is all figurative. In a literal sense, I have been suicidal;
Frequently spotting murder weapons, I can no longer be in denial
I know only I can save myself but sometimes I wonder if I am not my own enemy,
Am I the grim reaper in my visions posed as my rival?
I really hope that is not the case because if it is, then I must save me

Our Women

Let me speak briefly about our sisters – they are all soul healers,
They daily deal with heartbreakers, molesters & drug dealers
Yet they are still standing tall like they are never forced to fall at all,
Done a great number by us men by playing shady ball
We take them for granted and then we act shocked when they leave us,
Call them with harsh names, forgetting the love that they gave us
But anyway... this all about our beautiful women,
Perfect in their wrongs, with none of their flaws hidden
Exquisite trees of life who bear fruit of life in their wombs,
Voluptuous physiques that make you wish to see your tomb
Man, they are to die for, live for & kill for;
I mean, they are the portal from oblivion to life, the reason
we exist; are they unfit to live for?
Capturers of souls of men with breath-taking features,
Each time we are lost, they are the ones who assist in seeking us
I am talking about psychological, emotional & spiritual reaches,
Only these fragile beings can offer us reasons to tread on
when the world pretends not to needs us
So may we treat them right; like they deserve to be,
And if you dispute, do not hesitate to approach me!

Sthembiso Ayanda Shabalala

Athel Unfolded

Allow me to unfold the meaning & purpose behind Athel,
Just so I can assure you that it has nothing to do with peril
Unless you regard it as such – I am known to be a hazard to a bunch,
And I never speak nor act without reason, plus I follow a hunch
Anyway, 1st thing to know about the name is that it is my alias,
It was given to me by me to have purpose coupled with meaning, I am sure that is obvious
The intent was to have something meaningful to distinguish us,
While inspiring self-belief that one day I will win & be glorious
An Athel is an unwithering tree, regardless of what the season is;
It also means noble prince, but in my case King, depends on what your perception is
I have always had zero tolerance for the labels people gave me,
Only I can decide my own destiny, so I am the only one allowed
to pick what my name ought to be
Days are more like a paper, words & deeds like a pen;
So scribble your beautiful story & be stern
It is all in your disposal – choose what is self-preferable,
Live life through the lot's eyes or be someone you feel to you is desirable

www.ingramcontent.com/pod-product-compliance
Lightning Source LLC
Chambersburg PA
CBHW042340150426
43195CB00006B/115